FEB 1 9 2013

Write a
Graphic
Novel
in 5 Simple Steps

Jeffrey Edward Peters

Creative Writing
in 5 Simple Steps

Enslow Publishers, Inc.
40 Industrial Road
Box 398
Berkeley Heights, NJ 07922
USA

http://www.enslow.com

Library of Congress Cataloging-in-Publication Data

Peters, Jeffrey Edward.
  Write a graphic novel in 5 simple steps / Jeffrey Edward Peters.
    p. cm. — (Creative writing in 5 simple steps)
  Includes bibliographical references and index.
  Summary: "Divides the creative writing process into five simple steps, from inspiration to publishable story, and includes in-depth treatment of the graphic novel genre with writing prompts"—Provided by publisher.
  ISBN 978-0-7660-3888-2
  1. Graphic novels—Authorship—Juvenile literature. 2. Creative writing—Juvenile literature.
I. Title.
  PN6710.P413 2012
  741.5'1—dc23
                          2011026954

Future editions:
Paperback ISBN 978-1-4644-0101-5
ePUB ISBN 978-1-4645-1008-3
PDF ISBN 978-1-4646-1008-0

Printed in the United States of America

032012 Lake Book Manufacturing, Inc., Melrose Park, IL

10 9 8 7 6 5 4 3 2 1

To Our Readers: We have done our best to make sure all Internet Addresses in this book were active and appropriate when we went to press. However, the author and the publisher have no control over and assume no liability for the material available on those Internet sites or on other Web sites they may link to. Any comments or suggestions can be sent by e-mail to comments@enslow.com or to the address on the back cover.

Every effort has been made to locate all copyright holders of material used in this book. If any errors or omissions have occurred, corrections will be made in future editions of this book.

♻ Enslow Publishers, Inc., is committed to printing our books on recycled paper. The paper in every book contains 10% to 30% post-consumer waste (PCW). The cover board on the outside of each book contains 100% PCW. Our goal is to do our part to help young people and the environment too!

Cover and Illustration Credits: Cover and Book Key images courtesy Shutterstock.com; © Jeffrey Edward Peters, pp. 15, 24, 27, 36, 39–43.

Contents

Book Key

Keeping a Journal

On the Web

Genre History

Fun Fact

Check It Out!

Writer's Block

Here's an Idea!

Your Assignment

Organizer

Daydreaming

Step 1

Inspiration

By 1960, Stan Lee was sick and tired of comic books. He had been writing and editing for Atlas Comics for twenty years—since he was seventeen years old. At this point, he was just churning out formula horror tales, romances, and wild adventures of monsters from outer space. Lee was ready to quit and try something else. Then fate intervened.

Just as he was thinking about getting out, Lee's publisher asked him to create a new team of superheroes. While very popular in the 1940s, the superhero genre had been reduced to just three published characters for most of the 1950s: Superman, Batman, and Wonder Woman. But DC Comics had recently found success with superheroes again—particularly with their new superhero-team comic, *Justice League of America.* Lee's publisher wanted to jump on the trend and make a quick buck. Ultimately, Lee agreed to write the new superhero team . . . but only if he could do it his way.[1]

Using a new combination of science fiction, romance, and monsters, Lee and illustrator Jack Kirby created the Fantastic Four. The characters had no costumes, no secret identities, and argued just like a real family. The success of this new approach to superheroes led Lee unch *Spider-Man, Hulk, Daredevil, The X-Men,* and y other popular titles. Lee convinced his publisher to me the company "Marvel Comics," with himself serving as editor in chief. By treating superheroes as flawed people with everyday problems and failings, Stan Lee—along with his cocreators Jack Kirby and Steve Ditko—reenergized the genre and revolutionized the comics industry.

And to think, Stan Lee was just about ready to quit. It just goes to show that life, just like comics, has many surprising twists and turns. Opportunity and inspiration can happen any time, often when we least expect them.

Comics

Comics, also called sequential art, are currently a billion-dollar annual industry, with film adaptations of comics making more than $10 billion in the last two decades alone.[2] Bookstores have large sections dedicated to graphic novels, with separate shelves for children/young teens and for adults. Local comic-book stores and libraries are stuffed to the ceiling with paperback and hardcover collections of comics and manga.

Men and women working in the professional world of comics have lifelong careers doing what they love, combining words and pictures to tell stories and share ideas. In today's comic-book marketplace (represented mainly by Marvel and DC Comics), you need executives, a publisher, an editor in chief, an editor, a writer, a penciller, an inker, a colorist, a letterer, a printer, a marketing department, a distributor, and lots and lots of buyers and fans to publish a graphic novel. But for the purposes of this book, we will focus on the

What Is a Graphic Novel?

Comics language can be a bit confusing. For example, a "comic book" is not really a book; nor is a "graphic novel" really a novel. Books, whether paperback or hardback, are bound and have spines. Comic books, however, are stapled together. In reality, they're more like magazines than books. Still, the term *comic book* persists.

A novel is a work of prose fiction, usually between 30,000 and 100,000 words in length. Some graphic novels are similar to prose novels, but not always. Yet again, the term *graphic novel* persists. Any comic published or collected into book form is still, at this point, largely referred to as a graphic novel.

Pioneering comic artist Will Eisner coined the term *sequential art* to refer to comic art. He likely did this because the term *comics* was too widely viewed (in the United States, at least) as something just for kids. (It's likely the term *graphic novel* was invented for this same reason—because it sounded more adult and serious than *comic book,* and their creators were hopeful of reaching a more adult audience.) Sequential art is any art that tells a story through pictures that are viewed in an ordered sequence. All comic art can be referred to as sequential art or, more simply, a comic.

basics of writing and illustrating. Even if you find another artist to draw your story for you, you will still have to publish, market, and possibly sell the work yourself. In the comics community, this is known as being "independent," or "self-publishing."

‍efore You Start

If you already love to read and write, you're well on your way to becoming a comic writer or illustrator—especially if you like comic strips and comic books. But if all you read are comics, you're not going to be a very good writer or illustrator in any medium. As famous comic writer/artist Frank Miller once noted early in his career: "It's the duty of someone who works in a given form to study other related forms and bring something of them to his work. I've seen countless Alfred Hitchcock films, which provide a lot of material on different levels, including the use of light and shadow."[3] Miller was discussing his work as illustrator on the comic book *Daredevil*. Years later, however, he actually did work as a big-budget film director.

In addition to comics, you should sample film, television, novels, short stories, poetry, plays—every form of art, basically. Only by taking a wide sample of different art can you make informed decisions about how best to express yourself as an artist and create the best work you can. This holds true for all artists, really—but especially so for a comic artist. This is because comics naturally combine both text and images, two of the primary forms of artistic expression.

The genre possibilities are many. Superheroes and funny animals abound in comics. In addition, there are many autobiographical and biographical graphic novels. There's also horror, romance, mystery, fantasy, and science fiction. All these genres translate easily into the comics form. Some of the best comics will often combine elements from many different genres.

Comics Versus Film

Steve Gerber was a comics writer best known for his creations *Howard the Duck* and *Omega the Unknown*. Later, he also worked as a television writer. As they are both visual mediums, comics and film have some key similarities. But each also presents different challenges. An interviewer once asked Gerber about the difference between the two forms. Gerber responded:

> *Comics are much more difficult, in my opinion. In film, you're describing a continuous sequence of moving pictures to convey an action. In comics, you have to select the most dramatic and critical point of each action and then make those points connect in such a way as to give the illusion of a continuous sequence. The writer has to think about the visual elements very differently.*
>
> *Comics are also, as I mentioned earlier, much more a literary medium than film. The actual words receive more immediate scrutiny from the audience, simply because they're right there, in plain view on the page. And yet, comics dialogue has to be even more economical than film dialogue, because of the spatial limitations. No matter how many words a film character speaks, they won't cover up his face.*[4]

nic Strips to Comic Books

You can find examples of sequential art that were first etched in stone many thousands of years ago. But comics as we know them today began with "the funnies," or newspaper comics. The simplest form of a newspaper comic can be seen in one-panel comics such as *Dennis the Menace, The Family Circle,* or *The Far Side.* In this type of comic, your idea must be clear and concise. You have only one image and a few words in which to tell your story.

A more complex form of comic is the comic strip. Comic strips are usually three to four panels, so you have a little more room to share an idea, share a portion of a longer story, or tell a joke. Examples of either of these comics can be found in most daily newspapers, online, or in collections available in your local library, bookstore, or comics shop.

The first comic books were published in the early 1930s and were mostly reprints of newspaper comics. Eventually, comic books began to feature original material. The increased number of pages of the comic book would give artists the opportunity to offer readers longer and more complex narratives.

The Mechanics of Comics

Many writers can't draw very well, so they team up with an artist to collaborate. Usually a writer will create a script for each story, describing the picture in each panel and writing the dialogue for each character in the scene (like a play or movie script). The artist then uses this script to create the art for the book.

Whoosh! Zap! Blam!

One of the most fun elements of writing and drawing comics is depicting sound effects as words, which is known as onomatopoeia. There are words used to represent sounds, such as "Pow!" "Wham!" and "Krak-a-boom!" You can even make up your own words to represent noises and sound effects!

Comic dialogue is placed in word balloons, with tails pointing to the speaker. What a character thinks is placed in thought balloons—fluffy clouds with a series of circles leading back to the character. Story narration is placed in caption boxes, usually located at the top left hand corner of the panel. Some artists choose to have dialogue, narration, and thoughts flow freely around the page, designing the words to fit with the art. Some place the words above, below, or next to the art panels. Some use no words at all, and tell the story only with pictures. As you work, you'll find your own style and use what works best for the story.

Pictures

"A picture is worth a thousand words," the old saying goes, and that saying holds true in the art of comics. The best art tells a story, reveals the characters, and engages the imagination. Rather than describing what a person looks like, you simply draw him or her. Long passages describing location are painted or photographed instead. The style of art is not important as long the finished picture can be reproduced for publication. Writer/artist Matt Feazell has created hundreds of hilarious eight-page stories with his stick figure character Cynicalman. Artist Alex Ross paints all of his images using tempura, gouache, oils, or airbrush. As long as the style of artwork fits and enhances the story, the art can be in any medium or style and as simple or complex as the creator chooses.

Panels

In comics, pictures and words are combined in panels to tell the story. Each single panel is a window into the world the artist creates in his or her imagination. On a piece of paper, create a simple square box, large enough for you to draw a picture in. This box (or panel) is how the reader looks into your imagined reality. By carefully choosing the images, details, and text you place into this panel, you decide how much of what is happening in your world the audience will see at any given moment. By placing many of these panels one after another in order, you take the reader on a journey through that world. This is called "storytelling" and is the basis of all comic art.

The first page of a comic introduces characters, locations, and story to the reader. Most superhero comics begin with a splash page. A splash page is a single panel that fills one entire page. The pages that follow generally contain from four to nine panels of art and text, each capturing an important moment of the story to move the plot along. There can be more or less panels per page, depending on the demands of the story.

Much like viewing film or television, each [ ] at the world from a certain point of view (POV [ ] many different point-of-view possibilities. The l[ ] establishing shot, is a view from a distance. T[ ] shot is a view of characters from about the waist [ ] up shot is a very close view of a face or object, u[ ] to emphasize an important detail. The worm's eye view is looking up from below, usually done to emphasize the large size of something. The bird's eye view is looking down on a scene from above. A mix of all these different viewpoints will help make the story visually interesting to the reader.

What Are Your Themes?

When starting out, the most essential question for every writer is "what do I want to say?" Think about what's important to you and you will likely find your message, or theme. The theme of most superhero stories is good versus evil—but you don't have to limit yourself to just this. Your theme can be about happiness, fear, ambition, love, nature, death, alienation, religion, or politics. It can be about one person's journey, a fall from grace, or a triumph over some adversity. Choose a theme you are passionate about.

Inspiration Is Everywhere!

Remember to keep your eyes and ears open at all times. An idea for a story, joke, or character can come from anywhere! For example, artist Jerry Robinson created Batman's nemesis, the Clown Prince of Crime, after seeing a movie called *The Man Who Laughs* about a refugee with a frozen smile and by looking at a joker in a deck of playing cards. He combined the story and the image to create his own supervillain, The Joker, who has plagued Batman for more than seventy years.[5]

Jaime Hernandez has been writing and illustrating the "Locas" portion of the *Love and Rockets* comic for more than three decades. When he started professionally, he was inspired by real people. His two primary characters, Maggie and Hopey, were born out of "going to L.A. punk shows and seeing these little punk girls who I just fell in love with."[6]

Creative Exercises

Chronicling Creativity: Keep a camera, sketchbook, or journal handy as a way to explore ideas and record images. Make a sketchbook by folding four blank sheets of paper together and stapling the folded edge. In your sketchbook, take a joke you have heard and illustrate it using words and images combined. What works best to convey the joke, a descriptive sentence, dialogue, or a picture?

The One-Panel Comic: Try creating a one-panel gag comic (see Figure 1 for an example). Draw a friend or relative, and write something funny he or she said underneath. When you're finished, show it to someone. Did the person laugh? Or do you need to add more story details in the art to make it more understandable to others? Draw and write a few different single images to determine how much art and how many words you need to add or subtract in order to make it easier for your reader to enter and understand your world. Try seeing how few words or how little art you can use to tell your story.

Figure 1

Story Strips: In your sketchbook create a comic strip (see Figure 2 for an example). Take a story or joke you have heard and illustrate it using words and images combined in three panels. What works best to convey the story, a descriptive sentence, dialogue, or a picture? Draw and write a series of six comic strips, telling a week-long story.

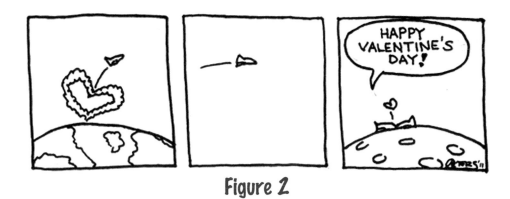

Figure 2

Step 2

Creating a Universe

Now is the time to create and populate your world. Stan Lee once said, "A writer is like God. He can destroy empires, create new universes."[1] In approaching your writing this way, you can create a powerful sense of verisimilitude in your work. Verisimilitude is the quality of feeling real.

Alan Moore is one of the most critically acclaimed comic writers in history. Among his many noted works are *V for Vendetta, League of Extraordinary Gentlemen,* and *Watchmen.* He endorses the world-building approach to writing. He once advised aspiring writers:

> *See the world your characters inhabit as a continuum with a past, a present and a future. . . .* Watchmen *was conceived in precisely this way. The story starts in October 1985 and ends a few months later. In terms of real time, that is the framework of the story, and I have all of the events within that period precisely worked out. In broader terms, however, the story concerns events going as far back as 1940, with individual sequences set in the '60s, the '70s, the '50s, the '40s . . . what we get an impression of, hopefully, is a world with a credible sense of depth and history, along with characters that share the same quality.*[2]

You don't have to go crazy outlining every last background detail of your characters and setting. But you should have a general sense of how your characters reached the point they're at when your story begins. You should have a clear picture of your world and how it has shaped your characters. Soon, your characters may begin to "write themselves." This means you know your characters so well you don't have to think about what they're going to do. The personalities you've given them make their actions obvious to you.

Sometimes you won't recognize this has happened until after the story is written. Neil Gaiman, author of *Sandman* and *Stardust,* once described it this way: "It's like you don't let yourself know you're going to kill this character later on. Then when you go back, it was completely obvious that you'd set everything up; everything's there, and it's the only possible way it could have gone. But you didn't know that it was happening that way when you were doing it."[3]

Character creation and design is one of the most fun elements of comics. It begins when you, as a creator, mentally become your characters as you draw them. Feel free to use parts of your own personality to create your characters.

Principal Characters

Good stories need a protagonist and an antagonist in order to create conflict. In a superhero comic, this is the hero and villain. Draw a picture of your character in your sketchbook. Add a cape and mask and he's a superhero. Add a spacesuit and she's an astronaut. Add a magnifying glass and he or she's a detective or a scientist. The more art you add, the more defined your character becomes.

Get It On Paper

Write it down. Take notes. Record your choices or you will forget them. You will refer to your notes later as you begin to edit your comic. Keep records of your ideas and images. Doodle to get your creative juices flowing. Build your art files with the pictures you draw. Search the Internet to find articles and images relating to your topic. Save them. Make a new sketchbook now and title it "Character Sketches." You may want to purchase a blank book from an art store or bookstore.

This also applies to personality traits. Is your character happy, mean, neat, or sloppy? Choose clear, simple adjectives to describe your character and write them next to your drawing. Redraw your characters to illustrate each of these traits. Make a page for each one of your major characters. Also consider your characters' inner desires and motives. What do they want? What do they like or dislike? Create two now, a protagonist and an antagonist. Make specific and unique choices for each character.

Secondary Characters

Now sketch and write notes for your supporting characters. These are friends, relatives, or coworkers of your two main characters. They can also be strangers, helping or deterring your principal characters from reaching their goals. Be specific about their relationships to your main characters.

Keep the design of these characters simple, so they can be instantly recognizable when they appear in your story. Background characters are simple caricatures used to populate your world. These can be doodles, outlines, or silhouettes. In designing and creating characters, it can be inspirational to use photographs as reference material.

The Plot

The simplest plots focus on a protagonist and an obstacle. More complex plots include an antagonist and a conflict. A story or plot outline is a list of what your hero does to overcome that obstacle. Good plots have a beginning, a middle, and an end.

Write out the key events that take place during the course of your story. Each event is known as a plot point. You can now sketch out some images and scenes with your characters moving from plot point to plot point. You can also create the plot as you draw each panel. This is known as unplanned creation, or improvisation. While creating your graphic novel, use both methods. Using a plot outline helps you remember where you are going as you write and draw your story.

Secondary characters have side plots of their own to reinforce the main conflict. Relate your side plots to your main theme whenever you can. Organize the story's plot elements by making an outline or chart. This will help you keep track of all your characters. You can use it to set up a complete plot outline for your story. Add or subtract scenes to move your story forward and reinforce your theme.

If something in your plot is not working, there's nothing wrong with changing it or even throwing it out entirely. Don't allow yourself to get stuck on one idea—many writers frequently change course in the middle of writing. Some even prefer writing "on the fly." Steve Gerber once observed: "Unlike some of my colleagues, I do not plot my stories months and months in advance. In fact, the 'next issue' blurb at the end of each story is always the most difficult line for me to write. I change my mind like some people change underwear."[4]

How Important Is the Plot?

The stories of the earliest comic books were usually very simple. Characters were not very deep and the object of the story was fairly straightforward. Writer Denny O'Neil, who started at DC Comics in the late 1960s, recalled, "Up 'til that point, almost everything at DC had been plot oriented. Characterization, if it was there at all, was secondary."[5]

So how important is the plot? These days it is not nearly as important as it once was. It is still essential as a road map for where your story begins and ends. But there are many other important elements to consider when writing. Alan Moore advises: "One thing that might be helpful to muse upon is what a plot isn't. A plot isn't the main point of the story or the story's main reason for existing. It is something that is there more to enhance the central idea of the story and the characters who will be involved in it than to dominate them and force them to fit its restrictions." He continues, "Coming up with a straightforward, mechanical plotline isn't difficult at all, and there are plenty of tried and tested formulas to fall back on, especially within the comic industry."[6] In a separate interview, Moore remarked, "The plot is as much a vehicle for the actual story as the language is, or the various other literary techniques. The plot is not what the story is about. It is something that is there purely to enhance what the story is about."[7]

Full Script Versus the Marvel Method

Once you've got your plot finalized, your next step depends on your working situation. If you're working with an illustrator, you need to decide how you are going to collaborate. There are two main ways of doing this: full script and the Marvel Method. Full scripting is when a writer creates a script that details all of the action, page by page, panel by panel, for the illustrator. The Marvel Method is when the writer gives the illustrator a plot and the illustrator decides how to draw it up. When he's done, the writer gets the fully drawn pages back and fills in the dialogue and captions.

The Marvel Method began with Stan Lee and Jack Kirby during their Atlas days doing horror and monster comics. As Lee recalled: "I'd be writing a script for [Steve] Ditko to draw. Jack [Kirby] would come in to drop off a job he'd finished and he'd want another script to start on. I'd tell him, 'I can't get you one now. I have to finish Ditko's.' But so that Jack wouldn't leave empty-handed, we'd talk out a plot and I'd send him off to draw it. That way, he'd have work, and after he handed the pages in, I'd write the dialogue."[8] Lee and Kirby continued to work this way when Marvel Comics got its start. Eventually it became the standard working procedure between most Marvel writers and artists.

If a writer wants more control over the story, he or she will usually work full script. Some writers like to give their artists very detailed scripts. Alan Moore is one writer particularly famous for this. For example, the first issue of the *Watchmen* comic book (the first chapter of the collected graphic novel) contains twenty-six pages of comic illustration. Moore's script detailing these twenty-six pages was, as artist Dave Gibbons recalled, "101 pages of typescript—single-spaced—with no gaps between the individual panel descriptions or, indeed, even between the pages. I know some writers always start a new page on a new sheet. Well, this just runs on and on and on and on for a hundred and something pages."[9]

Following the full-script method does not always guarantee that the writer gets what he wants, however. There was a particular story Denny O'Neil once wrote for *Batman* in the mid-1970s that serves as a good example. In those days at DC, the writer handed in a script to the editor, who would then assign it to an artist. The writer would often not see what the artist did with his script until after it was published. When O'Neil finally saw this *Batman* story on the comics rack, he got a surprise. As he recalled: "I wanted a real crummy diner, lower east side, with a couple of fishwives, and I get these well-turned out, well-coifed, elegant, upper-east-side women. I screamed to myself and said, 'why didn't somebody catch that?' I would have changed the dialogue if I had seen that picture. That's a point for working Marvel style."[10]

The Marvel Method would certainly tend to lend itself to more surprises of this nature. But some such surprises can be pleasant ones. One famous example of this is the character of the Silver Surfer. The Silver Surfer made his first appearance in a multi-issue story line that ran in *Fantastic Four,* later referred to as "The Galactus Trilogy." But he was not part of Stan Lee's original plot. As Lee recalled, "The [artwork] came back [from Kirby] and I could hardly wait to start writing the copy. All of a sudden, as I'm looking through the drawings, I see this nut on a surfboard flying through the air. And I thought, 'Jack, this time you've gone too far.'"[11]

The Silver Surfer was a happy accident. As it turned out, Lee saw something noble in the way Kirby rendered the character and he wound up playing a major role in the story line. Eventually the character would even star in a comic-book series of his own, which Lee would write. But their creative process raised questions that comic fans still debate today: how much credit for their work should go to Lee, and how much should go to Kirby?

Credit Where It's Due

If you choose to work using the Marvel Method with an artist, it is important to settle the issue of proper credit. Depending on how much the artist adds to your story as he's drawing it, you might want to give him credit as a co-plotter. This is what Lee and Kirby did with some of the later issues of *Fantastic Four.* (There were also times when a Lee-Kirby comic would be credited as "produced by Stan Lee and Jack Kirby" or "a Lee-Kirby production.") It is very important that everyone involved in your project receives proper credit for their work.

Creative Exercises

One Pager: Come up with a full-page story using any characters you can imagine. Use multiple panels. Add an obstacle, antagonist, or conflict. Make sure the story has a beginning, middle, and end.

Character Designs: Create your main characters by drawing them from front, side, three-quarter, and back views. Write down their key personality traits, dialogue ideas, or abilities on the page. Draw them in action! (See Figure 3 for an example.)

Figure 3

Step 3

Putting Words and Pictures Together

Writer/artist Scott McCloud once noted that in comics, "Words and pictures are like partners in a dance and each one takes turns leading."[1] You might have a great story, but if it is poorly illustrated, the experience for your audience will be lessened. Even if you are not drawing your comic pages yourself, you should understand how a good comic page is composed. If you're working full script, you will also be detailing page and panel layouts for your artist, so you will need to know some of the mechanics of page layout. You will also likely be editing your project yourself, so you will need to recognize what makes the art strong and what makes it weak. Any mistakes or inconsistencies with your storytelling goals will have to be marked and sent back to the artist for correction.

Making a Splash!

In comics, a panel that takes up an entire page is called a splash page. It is a showy and presentational panel that can be an effective way to introduce your world. In film, this is called an "establishing shot." Your character's location is "established" in this panel. It sets the scene. This panel can be used to introduce your characters and any conflicts between them. A splash page should include a title, dialogue balloons, narration boxes, and sound effects. It should also include creator credits and copyright information.

On every following page, you'll likely break your story into smaller, multi-panel pages. Using your plot outline from Step 2, create a thumbnail for each page of your story. (Aim for an eight-page story for now). Thumbnail sketches are small, quick drawings of a panel. Thumbnail each page to try different design ideas. Draw a panel for each action or plot point. Arrange your artwork, dialogue balloons, narration boxes, and sound effects in each panel. Design each page, and then move quickly onto the next page. Your panels can be of any shape and size, and you can place as many or as few on a page as you like. Panels can be architectural or natural frames used as a border. They can illustrate the mental or emotional state of your characters. Four to nine panels per page is the average, but feel free to experiment and find your own graphic style.

Thumbnails

A thumbnail should be as simple as you can make it. Each page is drawn about two by three inches in size, with dialogue, narration, and notes written off to the side. (See Figure 4 for an example.) They allow you to quickly create your images in micro-size. By working small, corrections and adjustments can be made easily. Use your plot outline notes and character drawings as reference while you work.

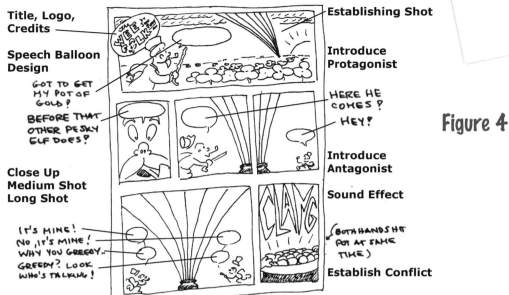

Figure 4

When drawing in panels, apply the rule of threes. Use small, medium, and large objects to indicate distance from the frame. Foreground, main action, and background details give a three-dimensional depth to your artwork. Try to include such details as animals, furniture, food, tools, etc. Keep your drawings simple, clearly showing what happens. You can improvise more panels as you create, but always refer back to your plot outline to keep your story on track.

As you write and draw, keep a few simple ideas in mind. The last panel of every page should contain an event that builds suspense, for example, the arrival of a new character or an unforeseen occurrence. This makes the reader want to turn the page. For standard comic books, generally speaking, every eight pages has a plot twist, and every twenty-four pages (the length of a standard comic-book story), has a major cliff-hanger ending. These techniques keep the plot moving and the story developing, and compel your reader to keep reading, anxious to discover what happens next.

Alan Moore on His Creative Process

"The first thing I do is work out the characters I have for the story and THEN make them fit into the plot that I have in mind. Then I try to roughly map about how many pages each section of the plot will take. Next, I divide each individual page into panels and draw totally inscrutable scribbles (understood only by me) that represent the figures and their actions. Once I get the story planned out, I go back and add in the dialogue. The final stage consists simply of talking it out loud.

It's a very straightforward process, but often during the working of a story, little extra 'sparks' pop up that add to the story's content. You have to be open to ideas."[2]

Beside your little thumbnail pages, quickly write down any dialogue or narration you want to include. On your thumbnail panels draw in your speech balloons, place lines for free-floating text, and include boxes for your narration. Words can also be placed beside or below your art. Write in sound effects. You can use these words as design elements in your panel.

The pace of your story is based on the amount of panels per page. Simple art and fewer words allow your reader to experience speed when reading. More words or art detail slows the reader down because they have more information to process. For now, draw only your plot points.

Some Tips

Illustrators: Don't worry about the quality of your art at this point. Draw your characters using simple stick figures. Use circles, squares, and triangles to indicate objects and locations. Try different shots (close-up, bird's eye, worm's eye, etc.) for variation.

Writers: This could be a useful exercise for you to try as well. Making thumbnail drawings, or larger ones with simple stick figures, gives you a good idea of how to pace your story visually. It might also allow you to nip potential problems in the bud and save your artist the time of drawing something that does not really work for your story.

Visit your local comic-book store or bookstore. Find a comic book or graphic novel you like. Study and examine how the artist and writer tell a longer story.

Creative Exercises

Thumbnail Check: Double-check your thumbnails to make sure the story is clear and your panel and page designs are clean. Will everything fit? Check your spelling and grammar on dialogue and narration.

Practice Panels: Choose some of your favorite panels to start drawing in more detail. Work in full size, adding art details and making sure the words fit in the panel.

Step 4

Finishes

If you are planning on illustrating your own work, the first trait you will need to have is patience. Even if you already have some artistic talent, it will take time and practice to get the hang of putting together a solid comic. When you compare your first attempts to published work, you will no doubt feel discouraged. Just keep in mind that the creators of those published comics worked long and hard to develop their skills. Their first comics were likely flawed as well. The only way for an artist to improve is to keep working at it.

Joe Kubert is another legend among comic illustrators. In 1976, he started the Kubert School, where many comics artists have gone to learn the craft. Kubert observed: "There are allowances that have to be made in teaching, where a student is allowed to make mistakes. I think it's important for a student to be allowed to make mistakes, so he can see where he went wrong and then change his mind. You can't really do that by telling them; it has to be seen and experienced."[1]

If you keep at it, eventually you should start seeing improvement. Artist Dave Sim tells young artists: "First you get good, then you get fast, then you get good and fast."[2] But again, it takes time and patience.

Another essential trait for an artist is discipline. Sim remembered when he was starting out that "in Southern Ontario alone there were a dozen guys who had success written all over them—guys with a natural ability, a smoother finish, better storytelling. . . . They would draw everything in the world except page one, panel one."[3] The most important thing is to get started. The second most important thing is to keep at it.

Illustrating in Earnest

Before you transfer your story to full pages, check your plot outline and make sure your thumbnail art properly tells your story. Now is the time to make changes, adjustments, and corrections.

Working Digitally

More and more artists today are abandoning pencils and ink to work digitally. (And just about all lettering and coloring are done digitally now.) Digital illustrators draw on tablets connected to their computers via USB ports and their art is saved directly to hard drives. The most common programs they work in are Adobe Photoshop and Adobe Illustrator, though there are others. Working this way requires specialized training and knowledge beyond the scope of this book. For those who want to explore the possibilities of digital illustrating, check out the Further Reading section.

Standard comics are published in a 6 x 9 inch format. You can create your art pages at this size if you choose. Some artists work larger, 10 x 15 inches, and shrink their art for publication, either by computer or photographically. A page of 8.5 x 11 inches can be folded in half and used to create a mini comic of your story, but it won't fit on a standard comic page. Graphic novels can be any size or shape, as long as each page of your story is the same size. Use any size you prefer, keeping in mind that it must be digitally photographed or scanned for reproduction at some point.

Jaime Hernandez on His Creative Process

"I used to draw only what interested me at the time. . . . 'Well, I know I can jump from here to here, because I know there's only a certain amount I can do here in the middle.' Sometimes it's the result of being bored with a page. 'I don't want to draw this now and if I make myself it's going to take too long and I'm going to waste time, so why don't I jump over here?' Then there are times that I want to get to that Maggie panel because she's dressed a certain way and I want to draw it.

. . . I know I need a page to tell a particular part of the story, but I don't know what I'm going to tell. So I leave that blank. And I still do it that way. . . . It's like a [musical] beat. I know there's so many beats that I'm going to need for something, but I don't know what."[4]

Use your thumbnails as a guide, and with a pencil and a ruler, draw your panels on your full-size art page. This is their final shape and size. Now, on your art page, write your dialogue, narration, and sound effects into your panels. Writing your words first determines how much room you have left in your panel for art. Draw your art around the words and begin to add details. The more precise your pencils are, the easier your inking will become. Penciling before inking your words and pictures allows you to make final changes easily. Once you've finished penciling all eight pages, double-check your spelling and make final pencil corrections as necessary.

Alex Toth may have some useful advice to offer at this stage. Toth was another of the great comic illustrators, starting out in comics in the 1940s before working in television animation in his later years. He was famous for his ability to show in just a few lines what other artists needed dozens of lines to accomplish. Toth would tell young artists: "What doesn't add, subtracts."[5] In other words, if what you're adding to your drawing doesn't make it clearer or say something new, it will take away from what you already have on the page. A more effective story can often be told with simplicity and clarity rather than with an abundance of detail.

Now it's time to finish your artwork. Get out some art tools! Apply ink over your pencils using a pen or marker. (This is known as adding inks or "finishes.") Ink your letters, words, and balloons first, making sure they fit! Then finish your artwork in ink. Be careful! At this stage of creation, you'll need white ink or paint to cover your mistakes.

The Creator's Kryptonite!

Guilt and pressure can be an artist's greatest enemy. Don't beat yourself up if your life gets in the way, and you don't achieve your goals at first. Keep working, learn your pace. Most importantly, enjoy the process!

When you've lettered and inked all eight pages, you've completed a short story in black-and-white sequential art. You can also add color, but keep in mind this will raise the expense of reproduction if you're planning on publishing in a conventional format.

Schedule your work, and then work your schedule. Set aside same time to draw every day, but be flexible! School and family obligations should always come first. When do you have time for creating? After school? After dinner? Are you most comfortable drawing at the dinner table or a desk? Set a goal for yourself. A professional comic-book artist completes an average of one page per day. Jeff Smith, writer and illustrator of the *Bone* series of comics, says he spends "a good three hours most days" at his drawing board, "until it gets into the deadline period, then it could be twenty hours a day for a week or two at a stretch."[6]

When you are finished, share your story with teachers, friends, and/or family. Take note of their questions and comments and consider how you will address them in future stories. Correct any mistakes or errors that are brought to your attention.

Creative Exercises

Picture a Word: The look of the text can influence what the reader mentally hears. Write a few sound effects, changing the appearance of the letters to illustrate the sound. Try drawing some dialogue the same way.

Judge a Book by Its Cover: Look at book and graphic-novel covers. Think what the story might be about based solely on the cover image. Design a cover for your project, including image, logo design for the title, and text.

Jeff Smith on His Creative Process

"I might jot down a quick list of four things that I want to have happen, and then I might add one of those ideas from my notebook. 'Oh, that's a neat moment. I want to get that in there.' I write down how I want to begin and how I want to end, and then I write an outline with a guesstimate of how many pages each thing will take. Then I'll start working out the comic on 8 ½ x 11 sheets of paper, writing and drawing at the same time. . . .

I move organically as I write. I can see the scene and the picture as I'm going, and that's what I'm drawing. I'm trying to lock in what I can see in terms of the composition—where someone is standing, what their expression is. I want enough of a drawing that I can tell those things, and then I write out the dialogue. . . . Sometimes I work straight ahead, but sometimes I'll work on a couple of scenes out of order knowing I have, say, a page and a half to get this idea across."[7]

Step 5

Publish!

Now that you have a finished story, it's time to share it with the world. This means reproducing your artwork pages for a larger audience. If you have a computer, scan them immediately, and then store them somewhere safe and flat. Or, you can start by making a simple mini-comic using a copy machine. Construct it the same way you made your sketchbook earlier, using two pieces of paper, folded over and stapled in half. (See Figure 5.)

Using the copier, reduce your art page until it will fit on half a page of paper. Do this for all your pages. Cut and paste your smaller pages onto four pieces of paper. These are your copy templates. Copy them using double-side printing, or flip the paper over in the tray to print again on the second side. Once you've copied your pages, put them together, fold them in half, and staple the edges. When you're done, you'll have a stack of comics to share, trade, or sell!

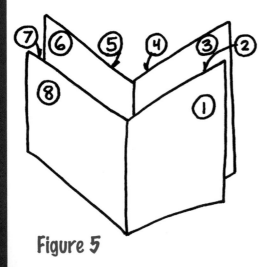

Figure 5

If you have a scanner and computer, you can set up your templates and print your own copies the same way. Number the back of your artwork pages and label your computer files with the page numbers for easy reference. If you have an art program on your computer and a color printer, you can now add color if you choose.

Once you've completed your story, there are many professional printers who specialize in printing comics and graphic novels. You may be able to find such a printer right in your hometown. There are also a number of online Web sites that print copies one at a time, on request. These sites charge more per comic, but you don't have to order as many copies. You'll need to upload digital copies of your pages and covers. Each site has a tutorial on how to submit your work for printing. Search for "comic-book printing" online to compare pricing and ease of use between Web sites. Perhaps one of your art teachers or English teachers can help you with this.

Web Publishing

The Web is a great outlet for comic creators that are just starting out. If you have a school Web site, perhaps they will put your project on it. Otherwise you will have to create your own Web site. Again, this would require specialized training and knowledge beyond the scope of this book. For those interested in learning more about Web publishing, please check the Further Reading section.

If your school has a manga or comic club, that's a great place to trade your graphic novels with others. (If one doesn't already exist, ask a teacher about starting one.) Have your club do a sale, selling the collected stories of your club. You can put any profit back into your club and expand it.

Selling your work in the larger world is complex business. Again, if you want to try it, work with a teacher or another adult. Together you can investigate setting up a vendor account with Diamond Comics Distributors, the largest comic and graphic novel distributor in the world. They have very specific guidelines for submission, which are available on their Web site in the vendor section. If you have a local comic store or bookstore, see if they might be willing to sell your work on consignment. Selling on consignment means that you get a percentage of your cover price after your books sell.

Get the Word Out!

Nothing sells better than good word-of-mouth advertising. You can expand your readership through marketing and promotion. Tell your friends, tell your family, and see if they want to buy a copy of your work. Attend local or national comic conventions. Here you can display and sell your work at an artist's table for a fee. You can also meet other artists and fans of graphic storytelling, who will share their ideas. Sell copies by listing them on Web sites like Amazon or eBay. Be sure to have your parents help you set up any necessary online accounts.

You have now entered the magical realm of comics. Enjoy your creative journey!

This opening splash page is designed to simply and effectively introduce the characters and setting of the story.

ONE DAY, SOME STRANGERS CAME INTO THEIR WOOD. A MAN MADE OF TIN, A MAN MADE OF STRAW, AND SOME FLESHY CREATURES THAT LOOKED RATHER GOOD.

This long shot of this top panel introduces what will be the main conflict of the story (Dorothy and her friends trying to make it through the Kalidahs' territory).

A LION WAS GUARDING THEM WITH A TOOTH-FILLED GRIN, SO THE KALIDAHS ALLOWED THEM TO WALK RIGHT IN.

YOU'RE AFRAID.

NO, IT'S A TRAP!

Most stories are told from the protagonists' point of view, but this story is told largely from the point of view of the antagonists (the Kalidahs). The fact that Dorothy and the other characters are so well known makes this easier, as they don't require much introduction.

Long shot, side view

Long shot, front view

Close-up, front view

Notice how it switches from a long, side view (panel 1) to a long, front view (panel 2) to a close-up, front view (panel 3). This offers some visual variety despite the fact that we're showing the same group of characters in each panel.

The last panel shows strong use of an illustrated sound effect.

Again, changing the point of view from panel to panel offers some visual variety.

Note how the action has consistently moved in a left-to-right direction throughout the comic.

Chapter Notes

Step 1: Inspiration

1. Stan Lee, *Origins of Marvel Comics* (New York: Simon & Schuster, 1974), p. 16.
2. "Comic Resurgence," *Junction,* April 2011, <http://www.junction-app.com/de/issues/detail/comic_resurgence-43.html> (December 4, 2011).
3. "Frank Miller: An Interview With the Young, Critically-Acclaimed Writer-Artist of Daredevil," *The Comics Journal,* No. 70, January 1982, p. 70.
4. Steve Gerber, "Fair and Fowl," *Sequential Tart*, January 2002, <http://www.sequentialtart.com/archive/jan02/gerber.shtml> (December 6, 2011).
5. "Look Out, Batman! It's the Jerry Robinson Interview!" *The Comics Journal,* No. 271, October 2005, p. 80.
6. "Pleased to Meet Them . . . The Hernandez Bros. Interview," *The Comics Journal,* No. 126, January 1989, pp. 76–77.

Step 2: Creating a Universe

1. Brooks Barnes, "Stan Lee Writes Himself Into His New Venture," *New York Times,* July 23, 2010, <http://www.nytimes.com/2010/07/24/books/24stan.html> (September 7, 2010).
2. Alan Moore, *Alan Moore's Writing for Comics* (Urbana, Ill.: Avatar Press, 2005), pp. 31–32.
3. Neil Gaiman, "The Hernandez Brothers Interview by Neil Gaiman," *The Comics Journal,* No. 178, July 1995, p. 99.
4. Steve Gerber, "Zen and the Art of Comic-Book Writing," *Howard the Duck,* No. 16, September 1977, p. 7.
5. Michael Eury, "An Interview With Dennis O'Neil," *The Justice League Companion* (Raleigh, N.C.: TwoMorrows Publishing, 2005), p. 127.
6. *Alan Moore's Writing for Comics*, p. 28.

7. Alan Moore, "The Alan Moore Interview," *Amazing Heroes*, No. 71, May 15, 1985, p. 41.
8. Mark Evanier, *Kirby: King of Comics* (New York: Harry N. Abrams, Inc., 2008), p. 112.
9. Dave Gibbons, "Dave Gibbons: Pebbles in a Landscape," *The Comics Journal*, No. 116, July 1987, p. 97.
10. Denny O'Neil, "The Alan Moore Interview," *Amazing Heroes*, No. 50, July 1, 1984, p. 104.
11. Evanier, p. 141.

Step 3. Putting Words and Pictures Together

1. Scott McCloud, *Understanding Comics: The Invisible Art* (New York: Harper, 1993), p. 156.
2. Alan Moore, "Dracula, Graveyard Poets, & an Interview With Alan Moore," *Vampirella / Dracula: The Centennial* (New York: Harris Publications, Inc., 1997), p. 44.

Step 4. Finishes

1. Joe Kubert, "Keeping Current With Joe Kubert," *NYC Graphic*, March 22, 2009, <http://graphicnyc.blogspot.com/2009/03/keeping-current-with-joe-kubert.html> (December 6, 2011).
2. Dave Sim, *The Cerebus Guide to Self-Publishing* (Kitchener, Ontario, Canada: Aardvark-Vanaheim, Inc., 2010), p. 67.
3. Ibid., p. 62.
4. "Pleased to Meet Them . . . The Hernandez Bros. Interview," *The Comics Journal*, No. 126, January 1989, p. 84.
5. Charley Parker, "Alex Toth," *Lines and Colors,* May 28, 2006, <http://www.linesandcolors.com/2006/05/28/alex-toth/> (December 6, 2011).
6. *Modern Masters 25: Jeff Smith*, ed. Eric Nolen-Weathington and Jeff Smith (Raleigh, N.C.: TwoMorrows Publishing, 2011), p. 79.
7. Ibid., pp. 79–80.

Glossary

comic—A form of artistic expression that typically combines words and pictures that are normally read in an organized sequence.

genre—A particular type or category of art or literature.

graphic novel—A term that can be used to refer to any comic art collected in a traditional book format.

improvisation—Creation without any preparation or plan.

manga—A Japanese form of comic.

medium—The form, vehicle, or mode in which an artist chooses to work.

narrative—Any story or account of events.

onomatopoeia—The forming of words or names based on the natural sounds they make.

plot—The plan of action for a work of fiction.

sequential art—Art that consists of a series of illustrations that are viewed or read in a specific sequence or order.

theme—A distinctive quality or concern in one or more works of fiction.

thumbnail—A small, quickly sketched version of a larger work.

verisimilitude—The quality of feeling true or real.

Further Reading

Books

Abel, Jessica, and Matt Madden. *Drawing Words and Writing Pictures: Making Comics, Manga, Graphic Novels and Beyond.* New York: First Second, 2008.

Guigar, Brad, et al. *How to Make Webcomics.* Berkeley, Calif.: Image Comics, Inc., 2008.

Scalera, Buddy. *Creating Comics From Start to Finish: Top Pros Reveal the Complete Creative Process.* New York: Impact, 2011.

Williams, Freddie E., II. *The DC Comics Guide to Digitally Drawing Comics.* New York: Watson-Guptil Publications, 2009.

Internet Addresses

Lambiek.Net
http://www.lambiek.net/home.htm

Comic Book Resources
http://www.comicbookresources.com/

Lulu.com—Self Publishing
http://www.lulu.com/

Index